D0893845

MILLBROOK ARTS LIBRARY

CRAFTS
FOR
EVERYDAY LIFE

edited by
Caroline Bingham
and Karen Foster

The Millbrook Press
Brookfield, Connecticut

Copyright © 1993 Merlion Publishing Ltd
First published in the United States in 1993 by
The Millbrook Press Inc.
2 Old New Milford Road
Brookfield, Connecticut 06804

Contributors:
Margaret Crush
Amanda Duncan
Heather Kingsley-Heath
Alison Leach

Designers: Jane Brett
            Tracy Carrington
            Roger Fletcher
Cover designer: Tracy Carrington
Picture researcher: Claire Allen
Typesetting coordinator: Gina Brierley

Printed and bound in Great Britain

Library of Congress Cataloging-in-Publication Data

Crafts for everyday life/Caroline Bingham, Karen Foster, editors.
    p. cm. – (Millbrook arts library)
    Includes bibliographical references and index.
    Summary: Examines such practical and decorative crafts as candle-
making, quilting, woodworking, and calligraphy in a historical context.
Includes hands-on craft projects.
    ISBN 1-56294-097-X (lib. bdg.)
    1. Handicraft – Juvenile literature. 2. Handicraft – History – Juvenile
literature. 3. Decorative arts – Juvenile literature. [1. Handicraft – History.
2. Decorative arts – History.] I. Foster, Karen, 1964–   . II. Series.
TT160.C74 1993
745.5–dc20   92-42944
                                                  CIP
                                                  AC

Artwork on pages 15 and 23 by Richard Berridge and on pages 6, 16
and 27 by Andrew Midgeley.

Models on pages 19 and 37 by Diane Barker; page 35 by Tracy
Carrington; pages 7 and 11 by Paul Fielder and pages 27 and 29 by
Sybil Gardener.

Photographs on pages 38 and 41 by Roger Fletcher and pages 4, 7,
9, 11, 12/13, 14/15, 19, 21, 23, 24, 26/27, 28/29, 30/31,
33, 35, 37, 38/39 and 42/43 by Mike Stannard.

CONTENTS

Clay pots

You can see from these clay samples that the color can vary from white to a deep red. All clay has to be cleaned before it can be used. Primitive people would have picked any twigs and stones out of the clay by hand, but today these and other unwanted substances are removed by machines. The clay then has to be wedged, which means it is pummeled, or kneaded, to make it elastic and to remove any pockets of air. In Ancient Egypt, potters wedged their clay by stamping on it!

Thinking about shape

Imagine you can pick up a lump of the clay pictured above. It feels cool and slightly damp to touch. You can squeeze, pinch, and roll it. Now imagine you want to make a pot with the clay. Before you begin, you will have to decide what your pot is to be used for.

Many of our most useful possessions are made from materials that have been used by craftspeople for thousands of years. You probably use at least some of these every day. Leather shoes protect your feet. Clothes made from wool and cotton keep you warm and dry. You drink from clay mugs. Then there's food cooked or eaten in pots made from metal and wood.

Clay is one of the oldest known of all natural materials. It is an earthy material made from particles of rock, so its color depends on where it is found.

The process of wedging clay

Designing a pot

The size, shape, and weight of a finished pot all depend on what the pot will be used for. Think about the pottery objects you use every day. It is easy to pick up a mug because it has a handle. Many cooking pots have lids that help to keep the heat and flavor inside. A jug will always have a spout, which makes it much easier to pour liquids accurately. Features like these are the basis of good design. The two pots pictured on this page both illustrate the fact that good design has always been an important part of the potter's craft.

A cooking pot

Can you think why this pot needed three legs? It is an ancient cooking pot, used for cooking over an open fire. The three legs would have kept it stable when it was standing in the fire. A clever idea has been included in the design. The legs of the pot are hollow to allow the contents to heat up more quickly. The deep scratches on the pot's surface are decorative, but they also increase the surface area that the fire can reach, so again, they make the cooking pot more efficient. Finally, look at the pot's wide neck. The contents would be easy to stir and to spoon out.

Hydria

This Greek water jar, or hydria, was designed to be carried on a woman's head when she collected water from a communal well. Look at the shape. Two horizontal handles made it easier to lift, while a third, vertical handle was used to tilt it.

A three-handled hydria from Ancient Greece

This cooking pot was made from clay over 3,000 years ago

Working with clay

Form a small ball of clay in your hands and press your thumb into the center to make a hollow, as in the picture on the left. You have made a pinch pot. Pinch pots were the earliest form of pots, and were certainly being made by cave dwellers some 13,000 years ago, if not even earlier! But pinch pots are small, and people soon began to look for ways of making larger pots which could be used for storage purposes.

Coil pots

The storage jar on the right is about 3,500 years old and stands over 3 feet (1 meter) in height. How do you think it was made? The storage jar was formed from sausage-shaped coils of clay, laid on top of each other. First, the potter would have rolled out a flat piece of clay as the base of the pot. Then, using coils of clay, the potter would have built up the sides of the jar slowly, leaving each coiled layer to harden a little before adding another. Jars of this size were shaped around molds.

You cannot see the individual coils of clay because the potter has smoothed the surface of the jar to hold the coils together. The completed pot was then decorated with pieces of clay, textured to look like lengths of rope.

A coiled storage jar from Ancient Greece

Heating the clay

By the time the storage jar was made, people had discovered that heating pottery to a very high temperature made the clay extremely hard. This process is called firing.

Methods of firing

Nowadays, pots are usually fired in electric kilns, but thousands of years ago, pots were fired in huge bonfires similar to the one pictured on the right. You can see the fired pots lying at the base of the pit. Before firing, the pots would have been covered with a thick layer of grasses and wood, but these have burned away in the picture, leaving just a layer of ashes. A pot that has been fired by any method will not soften again, even if it is soaked in water.

Make a coil pot

Making an unfired coil pot is a good way to learn to handle clay. You will need a small amount of clay. Remember to wedge, or work, your clay before you use it. Then flatten a circular piece of clay to use as a base. Roll out sausage-shaped coils with your hands and lay these in circles onto the edge of your base. One coil makes one layer, and its ends must be joined together. If you try to use a continuous coil for the whole pot, the sides will be uneven. Try and shape your pot as you go along. When you have finished, leave your pot in a warm place to dry. This will probably take one or two weeks.

This huge pit is a bonfire kiln in Mali

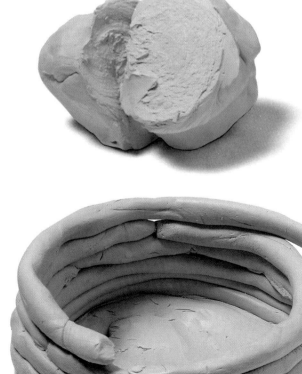

The potter's wheel

A Nigerian potter using a mechanical wheel

Some potters form their pots with the help of a revolving wheel. They throw a piece of clay onto the center of the moving wheel, then shape it with their hands. That's why we call this process "throwing a pot." Historians believe that the first potter's wheel was invented about 5,000 years ago. The invention brought exciting changes with it. Pots could be made so much faster on the wheel than by hand, and they had a more balanced shape.

Many modern potter's wheels are powered by electricity, but the first wheels had to be pushed around by hand. A round, flat stone was held off the ground by means of a stick through its center.

Using a foot wheel in India

Young apprentices kept the wheel turning and at the same time learned the craft by watching the potter at work. Gradually, potter's wheels were made that could be powered by foot, like the stone wheel above, leaving both the potter's hands free to shape and mold the pot.

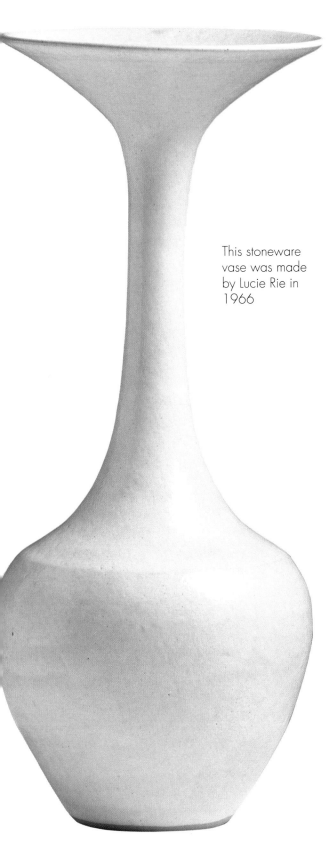

This stoneware vase was made by Lucie Rie in 1966

Fantastic shapes

The movement of the wheel allows the potter to draw a ball of clay upward to create tall shapes. This stoneware vase by the well-known Austrian potter Lucie Rie shows you just how elegant these shapes can be. Can you imagine Rie forming the base of her vase, then cupping her hands around the top to draw the shape upward into a long neck? It certainly isn't easy to work clay like this, but the shapes that result can be amazing.

Tools

Potters use wooden tools like those shown here to help them to work the clay on the wheel. A knife-shaped tool is used to trim away the thick wedge of clay that builds up around the base of a finished pot. The pot then has to be cut away from the wheel with a length of wire. Tools are also used by potters to decorate the sides of their pots.

A glazed Persian wall tile

Using flat pieces of clay

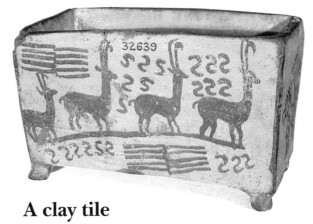

We have looked at some of the ways pots can be shaped, with and without the use of a wheel. But this oblong-shaped pot has been formed in yet another way. It is made from slabs of clay that have been flattened or rolled into sheets. One slab forms the base, and four slabs are brought together to form the sides. The simple decoration has been painted on with slip, a mixture of colored clay and water.

Can you think of another use for flat pieces of clay? Look around your home. Are there tiles on the floors or walls? Perhaps the roof is protected with tiles. Sometimes these are made from clay.

Making tiles

Tiles are traditionally made by pressing wet clay into plaster molds. The beautiful raised decoration on the Persian tile pictured opposite was formed when the slab of clay was pressed into a carved mold. The tile would then have been coated in a glossy finishing liquid called glaze and fired at a high temperature.

Glaze melts and sticks to the surface of clay when it is fired. It produces a shiny, hardwearing surface. Glaze makes the clay waterproof. This means that glazed tiles are ideal for rooms like kitchens and bathrooms.

This Egyptian slab pot is almost 5,000 years old

A clay tile

You will need some wedged clay. Turn back to the first page of this book to remind yourself about wedging. Roll the clay out on a damp cloth and then cut the edges with a knife to form a square or oblong tile. Use a ruler as a guide to make sure the edges are really straight.

Decorate your tile with patterned strips or balls of clay. You can attach these extra pieces of clay by brushing some slip onto both of the surfaces to be joined to help them stick. Scratch lines onto the surface of the tile, or use the end of a pencil to mark the tile with a pattern of dots. When the tile is completely dried out, you could paint it with poster paints and add a coat of clear varnish to harden and protect the surface.

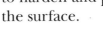

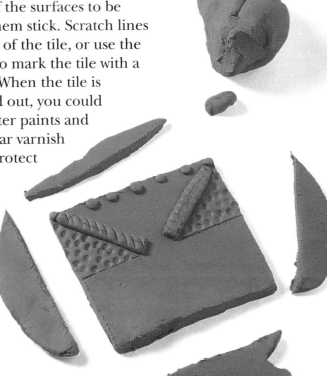

Carving wood

Just look at the variety in shapes and sizes of the tools on this page. They look so different that you might be surprised to know that they are all used for carving wood. Wood has been carved since prehistoric times. The first wooden bowls were probably made from a small wooden log, roughly hollowed out with a stone ax. Early carpenters probably used stone knives to smooth out the inside of their containers, too.

As people invented better woodworking tools, they were able to make smoother, more beautiful wooden objects. They learned how to carve wood into more and more useful shapes – from bowls and cups to chairs and tables.

Today, the simplest wood-carving tool is still the knife. Pocket knives are used to carve small objects into simple shapes using a process known as whittling.

Chisels and gouges

For more complicated carving, most woodworkers today use sharp tools called chisels, which come in various shapes and sizes. A chisel has a flat cutting edge to chip away wood in a special way, depending on its shape. A gouge is a kind of chisel that has a hollow cutting edge, in a u- or v-shape. The wood-carver uses a wooden hammer called a mallet to tap the chisel or gouge carefully into the wood and cut out a design.

A selection of wood-carving tools

A carved wooden door from Benin in Nigeria

Decorative carving

This Nigerian door is an everyday wooden object that has been carved into an elaborate and stunning design. You can see that the figures on the door are raised away from the surface. The wood-carver achieved this effect by cutting away the background wood to leave the design sticking out. This technique is called relief carving, and it is one of the most difficult woodworking techniques – especially when the design is as complicated as this one!

Carving in the round

Carving an object from a solid piece of wood is called "carving in the round." To carve a smooth bowl like this one, the shape is first marked on all four sides of the block of wood. The woodworker then carves around the main shape, cutting away the excess wood. Now the inside of the bowl must be gouged out and the outside shaped with a chisel. Finally, the whole bowl is smoothed with sandpaper and waxed or polished. This brings out the beautiful pattern of the wood, called the grain, so that the completed bowl looks its best.

Using machines to shape wood

To make a wooden cup with a long stem like the one in the picture below, the woodworker first fixes a long piece of wood onto the lathe. A pointed tool is then fitted to the lathe to bore out the cup's central hole. Next, the outside of the cup is shaped and smoothed with a series of different-sized chisels. This is called "turning the cup." Finally, the woodworker removes the cup from the lathe and polishes or varnishes the wood to bring out the grain.

A woodworker using a lathe

This woodworker is using an efficient machine called a lathe to create a chair leg with a completely smooth surface. The lathe just turns a piece of wood around and around, leaving the woodworker with both hands free. By holding a sharp tool against the revolving wood, the woodworker can shape the object evenly on all sides. The lathe can be fitted with several different tools, each of which has a special function in forming the final shape of the finished object.

A hand-turned wooden goblet

This man is using a bowdrill

Early woodworking

The lathe that was used to make the cup, or goblet, on the left, and the bowl that is shown here was powered by electricity. Can you think of ways in which woodworking machines might have been powered in the past?

The lathe is a modern version of various kinds of woodworking machines that were first invented thousands of years ago. One of the first of these machines was called a bowdrill. The picture above shows what a bowdrill would have looked like. As you can see, it was made from a hunter's bow. The bowstring was wrapped around a stick with a pointed end that was positioned on top of a piece of wood. The woodworker had to pull the bow from side to side very quickly, causing the stick to twist.

As the bow was moved quickly backward and forward, heat built up under the point of the stick, burning the center of the wood into a fine powder. When the powder was scraped away, a rough kind of hollow container was left.

The first lathe

As early as 2,000 years ago a version of the modern lathe called a pole lathe had been developed. This machine used a winding and unwinding rope to spin the wood against a tool. The movement of the rope was controlled by a foot pedal, so, for the first time, the woodworker had both hands free to control the turning process. Pole lathes were used in many countries until the invention of electricity.

This bowl was turned on an electric lathe

Wooden furniture

The Ashanti people of West Africa have a legend about a special piece of wooden furniture that belonged to their first king. The legend dates back to the time when the Ashanti were divided into fighting tribes, and in those days there was no king. One day a famous medicine man, Anotchi, visited Osai Tutu, who was the leader of one of the tribes. Anotchi announced that Osai Tutu had been chosen to be king of the Ashanti and that a sign to prove this would be given at a special ceremony.

So all the tribe leaders gathered excitedly together at a ceremony. Suddenly, a golden stool appeared from the sky and placed itself before Osai Tutu. The leaders were so amazed by this miracle that Osai Tutu was made king and the stool became his throne. The legend explains why small wooden stools are still important pieces of furniture in some regions of West Africa. They are all made in a special shape, to remind the people who use them of Osai Tutu's golden throne.

Part of the home

Wooden stools, chairs, tables, and beds are an important part of many homes. If you look around the place where you live, you can probably see many types of furniture. What style is your furniture? Is it light or dark wood? Is the design modern or traditional? Furniture is often made to suit its environment. For example, a solid oak chair fits well into a house in a cool northern country, but furniture woven from cane so that air can pass through it suits a hot tropical climate. So the style of your furniture often depends on where you live.

Simple or ornate?

Furniture is also made to follow fashion. This ornate wooden armchair was made to follow an English fashion of the 1660s. It has a richly embroidered silk seat cover and back rest. Look at the elegantly carved dolphin armrests and legs. The padded backrest means the chair is probably very comfortable.

A chair made by the Shakers

In contrast, this pine chair is very simple in design. It has a straight back, a cane seat and very little decoration. Simplicity like this is a common feature of furniture produced by the Shakers, a religious group who began to set up their own communities in North America during the 1700s. Shakers believed that furniture should be useful but not ornate. Many people prefer the simple shape of a chair like this to the more decorative style of the English chair. Which do you prefer?

This extravagant chair was made in the 1660s

Boxes

A Japanese inro

Have you ever thought about how often you use a box? Boxes for pencils, toy boxes, tool boxes, boxes for food, you probably use some kind of box every single day!

Large and small

A box is usually a four-sided container with a lid, but it can be round or oval. Craftspeople use all kinds of materials to make and decorate boxes – from wood or clay to silver or gold.

In Japan, small boxes like the one above are hung from the belt of a kimono. Traditionally, they were used to carry a brush and ink, but today they can be used to carry any small item. The boxes are called inro, and they are interesting because each one divides into four or five small compartments. These fit together so well that it is nearly impossible to see the joints once the inro is assembled!

Some boxes can be very large, like this wooden chest. Chests were one of the earliest kinds of furniture. They were used to store objects such as clothes and blankets or important papers. These huge boxes were often decorated with intricately carved designs.

A wooden chest

Interesting shapes

Not all boxes are made in simple shapes like squares or ovals. Many are carved in the shape of an animal or bird. Some are so cleverly made that at first glance you would not know they were boxes at all! This wonderful wooden hippopotamus is hollow inside and its top detaches to form a lid. It is an African box that has been carefully carved. It was probably used as a container for beads.

Making a treasure box

Make your own box for keeping precious things or souvenirs safe. First, collect together pasta shapes, sea shells, small pebbles and dried seeds. Think carefully about color when you are collecting these things. Apply a layer of glue to the outside of a plastic container with a lid (a margarine tub is just right). Think about how all the objects you have collected will look together. Then glue your collection onto the container, mixing colors and textures to create a good design.

Don't forget to decorate the lid, too. When the glue is dry, you can paint the inside of the box and lid in a bright color. Then varnish the box to protect it and bring out the colors of your shells and seeds.

This wooden box is from Africa

Glass

Stop and think about glass for a moment. You can see yourself in a glass mirror. You can look right though a glass cup. Things made of glass don't rot or rust. Glass must have seemed an incredible material when it was first discovered more than 5,000 years ago!

Today, we use glass in hundreds of ways in our everyday lives, from small utensils such as bottles, jugs, and bowls to car windshields and windows. In fact, glass is so commonplace that we almost certainly do not stop to think about how useful it is, or about how it is made.

Ancient Egyptian glass vessels

The Ancient Egyptians first made glass into small beads, but this glassmaking soon developed into a specialized craft. This Egyptian glass vessel was made more than 3,000 years ago. Look at the bold zigzag patterns. Each colored strip is a glass rod. The rods were wrapped around a sand or clay mold, one by one, to build up the shape of the vessel. Objects such as this were difficult to make and were very valuable.

A glass furnace in use

How glass is made

When sand and ashes are heated together at very high temperatures, they form a liquid with a thick texture like syrup. This is liquid glass, which is known more correctly as molten glass. Before it cools and sets hard it can be molded and shaped.

Blowing glass

The picture shows a blown-glass vase being made. The glassblower has collected some molten glass on the end of a hollow iron rod and blown very gently through the rod to form the glass into a bubble. While the glass bubble is still soft it can be squeezed, twisted, and pressed into different shapes using a wooden paddle and tools. This method of shaping glass was invented in Syria about 2,000 years ago. Suddenly glass was much easier to make, and as trade spread around the world, glass objects began to appear throughout Europe. People quickly saw the advantages of glass containers over wood or clay, and thousands of glass bottles were made to hold oil, wine, and other liquids.

The Portland Vase

This is one of the most famous pieces of glass in the world. It is well known because of the skill that was required to make it. The vase is made from two layers of glass. A design has been cut into the top, white layer, revealing the darker background. The vase is believed to be almost 2,000 years old. It survived until 1845 when it was smashed into more than 200 pieces! As you can see, the vase has since been carefully restored.

These tools are being used to shape the lip of a blown-glass vase

The Portland Vase

Clothes

When you get up in the morning, you have to decide what to wear. You might put on a T-shirt and a pair of jeans. Unlike many animals, you are not covered with a thick and protective layer of fur, so if it's cold outside, you will have to add a sweater, too!

Clothes made from hide

Human beings have always covered themselves to protect their skin from the weather and from scratches and scrapes. In early times, people were hunters. They were nomadic, which means they didn't have a settled place to live. They had to use the materials they found around them in the place they stopped to camp for food, clothing, and protection. When animals were killed for their meat, their skins, or hides, were scraped clean and kept to use as clothing and footwear.

Hide is a useful material for clothing because it is strong and flexible and can be cut without fraying. In cold climates, animal skins are used, complete with fur. The fur traps warm air and keeps the wearer snug, especially if the clothing is made with the fur on the inside. In hot climates the fur is usually removed. Sometimes the hide will then be decorated.

An American Indian buckskin belt

A North American Indian in traditional costume

Look at the belt on the opposite page and the clothes in the picture above. They are made from buckskin, which is the soft, flexible skin of the male deer. American Indians once used it to make all kinds of clothes, which were often decorated with colored beads.

Clothes made from plants

Do you have any clothing made from plants? Perhaps you have a straw hat, or a pair of summer shoes called espadrilles with soles made from grasses. Can you think of other clothing that is made from plants?

In the Pacific Islands, South America, and Central Africa, a special cloth called tapa, or bark cloth, is made from the bark of the paper mulberry tree. Tapa has been used to make clothes for hundreds of years in these places. Tapa is made from pounded bark. People often gather together to pound the bark on wooden boards.

When it is first formed, bark cloth is stiff, rather like cardboard. A specially carved beater can then be used to press a raised design onto the cloth. The cloth soon becomes soft and flexible. In Papua New Guinea, bark cloth is used to make skirts. Each skirt has three panels, and the bark cloth is painted with bold patterns. You can see examples of patterned bark cloth below.

Natural fibers

Cotton bolls

This is a stem from a cotton plant. The seed heads have ripened and burst open to reveal fluffy balls of cotton fiber. They are called cotton bolls, and if you could touch them you would find they are soft and springy. Look closely and you will see that they are made up of hundreds of fine fibers, tangled together.

After the cotton crop has been harvested, these fibers have to be brushed, or carded, so that they all point in one direction. The smooth fibers are then twisted to produce a strong cotton thread that can be woven into fabric in a process called spinning.

Spinning

The craft of spinning dates back many thousands of years. Today most spinning is done by machine, but some people still spin cotton by hand. The women in the picture below are using an ancient method of spinning cotton thread. The basket contains cotton bolls. The woman on the left is carding the raw cotton to remove small impurities such as twigs and leaves, and to straighten the fibers. The woman on the right is twisting a stick called a spindle with her right hand and feeding cotton onto it. As she does this, she gently twists the fibers into thread with her fingers.

Hand-spinning cotton in Africa

Silk

Silk was discovered more than 4,000 years ago by the Chinese. They kept the method of making silk a secret for 3,000 of those years, so that the silk they sold abroad, mostly to Europe, remained valuable. In fact, it became so precious and people thought it was such a beautiful fabric that it become known as the queen of textiles.

The silkworm

Silk is an unusual natural fiber produced by the silkworm when it is ready to turn into a moth. At this stage, each worm spins a covering, or cocoon, around itself. The cocoon is made of one strand of fiber called a filament which the worm wraps around and around itself. You can see a picture of a silkworm just beginning to spin a cocoon below. The filament from just one cocoon may be almost 3,000 feet (900 meters) long! To make silk thread, the cocoons have to be unraveled. The silk

This man is making a silk sari

does not need to be spun, unless the cocoons are damaged and the thread is broken, but a number of filaments have to be twisted together to make one thread of silk because each single filament is so fine.

Silk is woven just like any other thread. The best fabric woven from silk is so fine that, in India, a silk sari, which is never shorter than 23 feet (7 meters) long, can be scrunched up into a tiny ball small enough to fit into an adult hand!

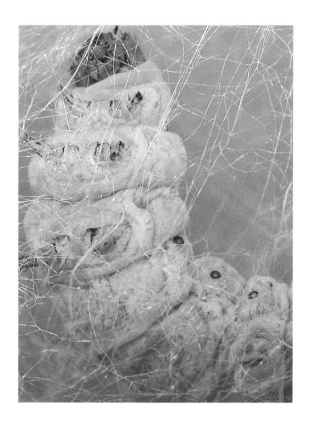

A silkworm spinning a cocoon

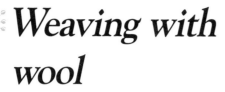

Weaving with wool

Sheep, llamas, and goats are covered with a thick, fleecy coat of hair called wool. We have already looked at the ways natural fibers are spun together to produce one continuous thread. Wool needs to be spun in the same way before it can be used to produce fabric. The picture on this page shows raw wool being fed onto a spindle to make a thread. The thread is now ready to be woven or knitted.

Most rugs and blankets are made completely, or partly, from woven wool. The craft of weaving is an ancient one. The Romans wove woolen cloaks almost 2,000 years ago and wore them for protection from the wind and rain.

What is weaving?

Weaving is the process of passing horizontal threads called weft threads over and under vertical, or warp, threads that run the length of the fabric. It is the warp threads that determine how long and how wide the fabric will be.

The back-strap loom

A weaver uses a frame called a loom to keep the warp threads tight and straight. There are many different types of looms, but one of the oldest is the back-strap loom. The woman in the picture is using a simple back-strap loom. She has tied the top ends of the warp threads to a point above her, and the other ends to a belt around her waist.

The sticks you can see in the fabric are there to help with the weaving. Each weft thread must pass over one warp thread and under the next. It would take a very long time to do this by hand. The bottom stick is left between the threads just like a weft thread. It holds the threads apart. The top stick is laid on top of the thread and is tied by fine thread to every other warp thread. All the weaver needs to do is lift the stick, pass the weft thread underneath and then drop the stick and pass the weft thread back.

Weave a mat

Make a simple loom from a piece of cardboard about 7½ inches (20 centimeters) square. Cut notches into the top and bottom of this cardboard. Fasten one end of a strand of wool to the back with sticky tape and feed the wool up and down the cardboard between the notches. These are your warp threads. Use a safety pin to thread a piece of wool over and under the warp threads. Work from the bottom of the cardboard to the top, and use a comb to push the lines of weaving tightly together. When you finish, unhook the wool from the notches and knot the ends together.

Weaving with a back-strap loom

Knitting

The Knitting Madonna was painted in the 1400s

Can you think of a craft that makes fabric using just yarn and two sticks? It's knitting, of course – a craft that is enjoyed throughout the world. No one knows exactly when knitting began, but a legend from the Christian religion says that Eve knitted the patterns on the serpent's back in the Garden of Eden as far back as the beginning of time!

Knitting in the past

It is thought that knitting began almost 2,000 years ago in Arabia, and spread to other countries along trade routes. Knitting became very popular in Europe in the 1400s, which was when this religious picture was painted. It is believed to be the first painting of someone knitting. Many knitters at this time were men who, after training for six years became members of special groups called guilds.

Today in countries like Peru it is still the men who knit, while the women weave. On the Island of Taquile on Lake Titicaca in Peru, a boy must knit his first hat at the age of nine without making any mistakes. This isn't nearly as easy as it sounds – the boys must knit complicated patterns, which have many meanings. Some patterns can even tell other people exactly where the wearer of the hat comes from.

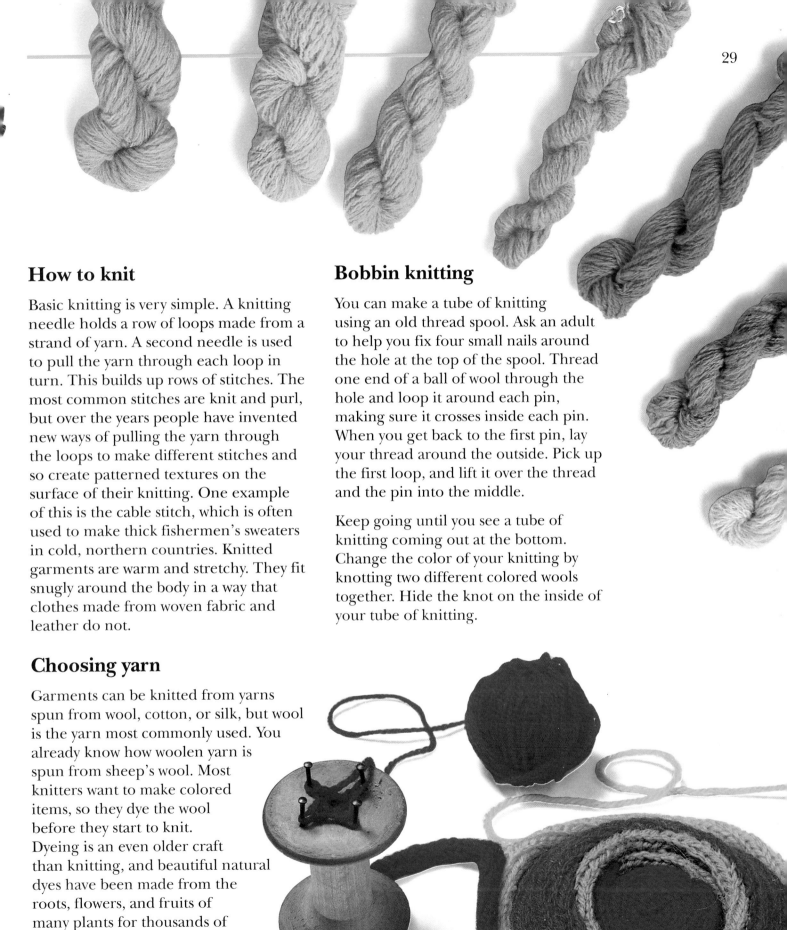

How to knit

Basic knitting is very simple. A knitting needle holds a row of loops made from a strand of yarn. A second needle is used to pull the yarn through each loop in turn. This builds up rows of stitches. The most common stitches are knit and purl, but over the years people have invented new ways of pulling the yarn through the loops to make different stitches and so create patterned textures on the surface of their knitting. One example of this is the cable stitch, which is often used to make thick fishermen's sweaters in cold, northern countries. Knitted garments are warm and stretchy. They fit snugly around the body in a way that clothes made from woven fabric and leather do not.

Bobbin knitting

You can make a tube of knitting using an old thread spool. Ask an adult to help you fix four small nails around the hole at the top of the spool. Thread one end of a ball of wool through the hole and loop it around each pin, making sure it crosses inside each pin. When you get back to the first pin, lay your thread around the outside. Pick up the first loop, and lift it over the thread and the pin into the middle.

Keep going until you see a tube of knitting coming out at the bottom. Change the color of your knitting by knotting two different colored wools together. Hide the knot on the inside of your tube of knitting.

Choosing yarn

Garments can be knitted from yarns spun from wool, cotton, or silk, but wool is the yarn most commonly used. You already know how woolen yarn is spun from sheep's wool. Most knitters want to make colored items, so they dye the wool before they start to knit. Dyeing is an even older craft than knitting, and beautiful natural dyes have been made from the roots, flowers, and fruits of many plants for thousands of years. The wools on this page have all been dyed with natural dyes. The soft shades of color are perfect for hand-knitted designs.

Rag rugs

An American
hooked rag rug

Can you think of a useful object you could make from the scraps of material on this page? You may be surprised that beautiful rugs like the ones pictured started off as scraps like these. A rag rug can be made from scraps of worn-out clothes or even old sheets. There probably isn't a cheaper way to cover a floor and keep a room warm! This proud lion is a hooked rag rug crafted in the United States. It shows you that quite complicated pictures can be made using this simple technique. The surface is smooth and neat, so the fine details of the lion's fur, the flowers, and the birds show up well. Would you like to look at this lion on the floor of your own room every day?

Hooking a rug

Making a rug like the lion rug from rags is quite simple. Old pieces of fabric are first cut into rectangular strips. The greater the variety of color and pattern on the strips the better, since obviously the finished rug will look brighter and more interesting. A piece of burlap is then cut to make the backing of the rug. Each piece of fabric is pushed through several holes in the burlap from the back with a rug hook like the one on the left. This makes a series of smooth loops. The cut end of the strip is hidden at the back of the burlap.

A prodded rug

This multi-colored rug is made in a different way. It has a shaggy texture, almost like animal fur. The maker poked strips of fabric just like those used for a hooked rug through the burlap, but looped each one only once, at the back. This leaves two cut ends on the front of the rug. Look at how groups of strips in shades of the same color have been fastened together to create a rainbow effect. A decorative fringe finishes off the rug.

Make a prodded rag mat

You will need a rectangular piece of burlap, about $9\frac{1}{2}$ inches (25 centimeters) long and $4\frac{1}{2}$ inches (12 centimeters) wide. Draw a design onto it. Next, cut lots of strips of fabric about $\frac{3}{4}$ inch (2 centimeters) wide and $2\frac{1}{2}$ inches (7 centimeters) long, and follow the instructions to loop each strip once at the back. Now carry on until you've finished your design, but leave a $\frac{3}{4}$-inch (2-centimeter) border around the edges.

Turn the border edges under and stitch them down.

This prodded rug was made by the English rug maker John Hinchcliffe

Patchwork and quilting

Tumbling blocks, rail fence, bear's paw, garden patch, log cabin, bachelor's puzzle. Can you guess what these wonderful names describe? They are all names for patterns found on patchwork quilts. You can see examples of the log cabin pattern and the tumbling blocks pattern on this page. Patchwork is scraps of material sewn together to make a large piece of material. A quilt is two pieces of material with a layer of padding in between, sewn together with intricate patterns of stitches. The padding traps air so that the quilt forms a thick, warm bedspread.

A log cabin patchwork quilt

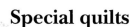
A tumbling blocks patchwork quilt

Special quilts

In the 1700s, patchwork was a popular craft among the settlers who arrived in North America from Europe. They had few possessions, and patchwork was a good way of using scraps of worn-out clothing to make a new, useful, object. It became a tradition to make patchwork quilts as gifts for weddings, christenings, and new homes, and women would gather together to share the work. These work days were known as quilting bees and, because the farms and homesteads were often many miles apart, they were also opportunities to have a long chat and exchange family news.

The younger women and girls would sew the patchwork pieces together while the older and more experienced women would quilt the patchwork top, padding, and plain fabric lining together. The quilting patterns were often complicated and were carefully worked with fine needlework stitches. It is amazing to think that groups of these creative women could produce large and beautiful quilts in as little as one day!

Other interesting uses

Patchwork that has been quilted makes an incredibly strong fabric. This strength means that it is ideal as a protective covering for people and animals. This patchwork is a suit of armor made in Africa. Today, it is only used for ceremonial occasions, but in the past its thick wadding protected horses from spears and knives in real battles.

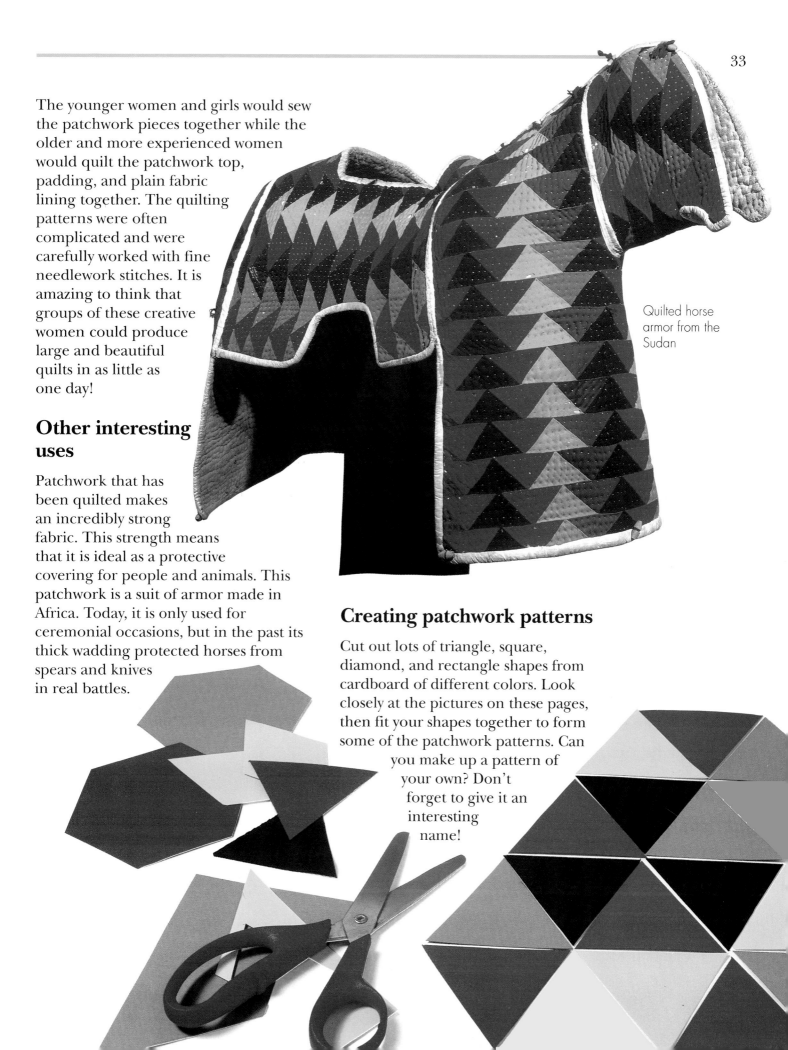

Quilted horse armor from the Sudan

Creating patchwork patterns

Cut out lots of triangle, square, diamond, and rectangle shapes from cardboard of different colors. Look closely at the pictures on these pages, then fit your shapes together to form some of the patchwork patterns. Can you make up a pattern of your own? Don't forget to give it an interesting name!

Making shoes

Roman leather shoes

What kind of shoes do you usually wear? If you live in a hot country, you might wear sandals with open straps to keep your feet cool. These Roman leather sandals were made almost 2,000 years ago. They show the development of a thick base to the shoe, called a sole, and an open top that is similar to many modern sandals.

Shoes soon became an important part of fashionable dress, and styles often changed. Some had high heels, some low. Some had rounded toes, and some sharp points. Most shoes were made from leather, but gradually materials like richly embroidered silk and linen were introduced. In many countries, thick soles of wood or metal were made to be tied onto delicate shoes to protect them while the wearer was walking outside. These were called "gels sandals" in China and Japan and "pattens" in England.

Handmade shoes today

Some shoes are still handmade today. Delicate embroidery and beadwork have been stitched onto the shoes below by hand. Extravagant shoes such as these are only suitable for very special occasions such as weddings.

Handmade shoes by Emma Hope

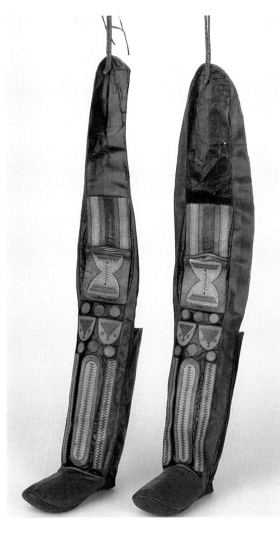

Nigerian leather boots

These leather boots come from Nigeria. Why do you think they would be needed in such a hot country? They protect the wearer from scratches or snake bites when walking or hunting. These boots probably belonged to a chief. They are beautifully decorated.

Make a pair of felt slippers

Draw the outline of one of your socks onto a piece of thick cardboard, adding a 1-inch (2.5 centimeter) margin. Trace this shape onto four pieces of felt. Lay two felt shapes together and stitch all the way around, leaving the top open so that you can put your foot into the slipper. Then turn the slipper inside out so that the stitching is hidden.

Repeat the process using the other two pieces of felt to make a slipper for the other foot. You could decorate your slippers with embroidery as in this picture. You could even sew on bells for your toes!

Long boots

In cold climates, thick leather and fleecy linings are used to keep the legs and feet warm. In Iceland, boots called mutakas are made of reindeer skin stuffed with dry grass. Long boots protect our legs as well as our feet.

Basket making

The Ojibwa Indians from North America have a legend that describes how the seven stars we call the Pleiades used to visit Earth disguised as seven beautiful sisters. The girls would descend in a decorated basket made of rushes and large enough to hold them all. They only stayed to dance on the shore of a lake, then climbed back into their amazing basket to rise up into the sky again.

Myths similar to this one are told around the world, showing us that basketry has been a popular craft practiced for thousands of years and in all parts of the world. Baskets are used as containers to hold all sorts of objects. Basketwork has also been used to build boats, and even houses. People weave baskets with many kinds of materials, from leaves, grass, and rushes to bark and twigs. This Kenyan woman is weaving with rushes. In fact, as long as a material bends enough to be woven, it can be used to make a basket.

An American Indian coiled basket

A Kenyan woman weaving a basket

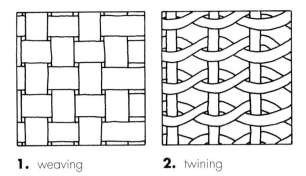

1. weaving

2. twining

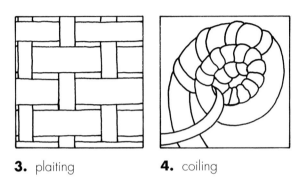

3. plaiting

4. coiling

Different patterns

These diagrams show you that there are four main basketmaking methods: weaving, twining, plaiting, and coiling. The North American Indians made beautiful baskets using the twining and coiling methods. The basket on the opposite page has been coiled and the designs made using different colored materials. The design on this basket celebrates the hunter. Some of these American Indian baskets were woven so tightly that they could be used to carry water!

Weave a basket

Unlike many crafts, intricate baskets cannot be made on a machine – a machine just hasn't been invented that can match the technique of skilled basketmakers! You can try your hand at weaving a basket using a square of cardboard about 7½ inches (20 centimeters) wide and 7½ inches (20 centimeters) long, and string.

First, decorate one side of a square piece of cardboard with crayons. Turn the cardboard over and mark another smaller square in the center. This is the base of your basket. Cut away the corners to leave a cross shape, and then cut each of the four sections into strips. Fold the cut sections up so that the pattern you colored is on the outside.

Now begin weaving with string. Pass it over and under each strip, around and around until you are ¾-inch (2 centimeters) from the top. Then fold the top of the cardboard strips into the basket, tucking them into your weaving to stop the string from unraveling.

Candles

Most candles today are made from paraffin wax, but this was not discovered until the 1850s. Before this, candles were made from an animal fat called tallow. Hollowed-out stones filled with tallow were used as lamps many thousands of years ago. Cave dwellers probably saw that tallow burned when it dropped onto cooking fires. At some point, people began to dip rushes into tallow to make a wick, which absorbs the wax to stay alight.

Timekeeping

Candles can also be used to tell the time! In the past, candles were produced with marked sections to represent hours. In England in the 1800s, bidding times at auctions were measured using candles. A pin was stuck into a candle at a specific point, and when the candle burned down and the pin dropped out, people knew the auction was over!

Making candles

Most candles are made using a mold. The wick is first put into a mold by hanging it from the top. The liquid wax is then poured in and left to harden.

A candle is a good source of light

At night, after the sun has set, we need to use another source of light to help us to see. Many houses around the world now have electric light, which brighten a room at the flick of a switch. But another, more simple form of lighting is still widely used. It is candlelight.

Making molded candles

Dipped candles

Candles can also be made by the dipping method. Long, fabric wicks are hung over a stick and dipped into melted wax. Each time the wicks are pulled up, another layer of wax has stuck to them. The wax is left to harden, and then the candles are lowered into the wax again. Repeated dippings build up the thickness of the candles. Look at the two candles below. You can see that they have been dipped into different colored waxes, beginning with dark blue and finishing with red.

Beeswax candles

These candles have been made from beeswax. Beeswax is the substance bees make to build their honeycombs. To form wax, the bees need to eat honey, which they make from nectar. Bees would have had to eat about eight ounces of honey to produce enough wax to make the taller candle on this page!

Beeswax candles are special because they do not smoke when they burn, and they have a pleasant smell of honey. Monks have used beeswax instead of animal fat to make candles for hundreds of years. To make the candles, the honey has to be removed, and then the wax melted. It is poured into molds to make sheets of honeycomb, and these are then rolled up to form the candle. It is a much longer process than making a dipped candle and needs careful skill.

Metalwork

A design was then engraved onto the back of the mirror. Metalworkers had discovered long before this that heat had an amazing effect on metal. In fact, bronze can only be made when tin and copper are heated and the two liquid metals mix together. Metals made from mixtures like this are called alloys. Bronze became such a popular metal when it was first discovered about 4,500 years ago that we call this time the Bronze Age. It was often hammered into weapons like these ax heads.

Two Bronze Age ax heads

This engraved bronze mirror is 2,000 years old

How many metals can you name? Gold, silver, and copper are three of the most commonly known. But did you know that a metalworker setting out to make an everyday object like a jug or a bowl has over 70 different metals to choose from? This is very different from a time some 7,000 years ago when people knew of only two metals, gold and copper! These were part of the Earth's rocks and could both be found among stones and dirt in river beds.

Bronze

The bronze object above is a mirror. A metalworker made it over 2,000 years ago, using heat to soften the metal and a hammer to beat it into shape.

Metalworking

Metals are still heated and hammered into shape by hand. The picture on the right shows a man shaping a metal bowl with a heavy mallet. He is holding the bowl with a long pair of metal tongs. He has to work quickly while the hot metal is still soft.

In the Bronze Age another method of heating metal was invented. It is called metal casting. Molten metal is carefully poured, or cast, into a mold, then cooled until it is hard. Casts can be made from stone, clay, or metal.

Shaping a metal bowl in Thailand

A pair of pewter tankards

Pewter

The Ancient Romans mixed tin and lead or copper together to make another alloy called pewter. This metal was very popular in Europe during the 1550s, when it was used to make a type of heavy drinking cup called a tankard. These pewter tankards were cast in a mold and then finished with a hammer.

Making a glass vase

To begin making a glass vase, the glassblower first picks up some runny, or molten, glass on the end of a glass rod called a blowing iron. Now he has to shape the glass. He rests the blowing iron on the chair, which is the name for the special kind of workbench he uses. Then he turns the rod and shapes the glass, using a wad of wet paper.

Adding air

The glassblower creates the hollow in the center of the vase by blowing hard into the iron. He covers the end of the iron with his thumb so that the air is pushed down into the glass.

Once a small bubble of air has formed in the glass, he blows down the iron again to increase the size of the hollow. This process is called thumbing out. Next, the glass is reheated in the central furnace, which is called the glory hole. The glassblower returns to the chair and forms the bubble of glass into the shape he wants with the two metal blades of the glassmaker's tools.

Blowing down the blowing iron

Shaping the rim

The glassblower cracks the vase off the blowing iron and transfers it to another rod called the punty iron. After heating the glass in the glory hole again, he shapes the rim at the chair before removing the glass from the punty iron.

Finally, the vase is placed in another oven called a lehr. This heats the glass just enough to change the chemical composition of the glass so that it becomes stronger without losing its shape. The vase is left in the lehr all day then allowed to cool slowly overnight.

1. Shaping the glass at the chair

2. Blowing the glass

3. Reheating the glass in the glory hole

4. Cracking the glass off the blowing iron

5. Shaping the rim of the vase at the chair

Crafts for sale

Many craftspeople work at their craft to make a living, which means that they have to sell the objects they produce. Imagine you are a craftsperson like this weaver. How would you go about selling your work? It might not be easy. If you live and work in a remote area, a sign outside your door wouldn't be much help. It's better to advertise your work by putting it on show, like this colorful display of rugs.

A weekly visit

In many countries, markets are a good place for craftspeople to sell their work. Customers will often travel quite a long way to visit a weekly or monthly market, and they will be in the mood to buy. All the craftworkers have to do is to pay for the stalls, and spend time creating an attractive display. If they sell enough at one market, they may be able to spend the rest of that week working on new objects instead of worrying about selling.

You may have seen stalls like this one in places you have visited for a day out or a holiday. Tourists are good customers for a craftsperson because they often want to take home something to remind them of their day. An object handmade locally is an ideal souvenir.

Shops and galleries

Finally, craftspeople sell their work in shops and galleries. The shop owner often has a wide variety of work to choose from, so the craftsperson's work has to be of a high standard to be chosen. And then the owner will take a percentage of the money whenever an object is sold, to pay the costs of running the shop. So next time you see a handmade object that seems expensive in a shop, don't forget that only part of that money eventually reaches the person who originally made the object!

A pottery market in Portugal

Index

Acknowledgments

The publishers would like to thank the following for permission to reproduce these photographs:

The American Museum, Bath for Shaker chair (page 17); lion rag rug (page 30); log cabin quilt (page 32) and tumbling blocks quilt (page 32). The Ancient Art and Architecture Collection for Portugese pottery market (page 45). The Ashmolean Museum, University of Oxford for Bronze Age axe head (page 41). Bristol Museum for Egyptian glass vessels (page 20). The Trustees of the British Museum for three-legged cooking pot (page 5); coiled storage jar (page 6); Egyptian slab pot (page 11); quilted horse armor (page 33); Nigerian leather boots (page 35) and bronze mirror (page 40). Cephas for American Indian costume (page 23); making molded candles (page 39) and making a metal bowl in Thailand (page 41). Christie's for buckskin belt (page 22). Bruce Coleman for making a silk sari (page 25); silk worm (page 25) and weaving rugs in Guatemala (page 44). The Crafts Council Collection for rag rug by John Hinchcliffe (page 31). Craft Suppliers Ltd. for tools (page 12); woodworker using a lathe (page 14) and ash bowl (page 15). His Grace the Duke of Norfolk for wooden chest from Arundel Castle (page 102). Fitzwilliam Museum, Cambridge for hydria (page 5). Hamburger Kuntshalle, Hamburg for *The Knitting Madonna* (page 28). Michael Holford Photographs for The Portland Vase (page 21). Emma Hope for wedding shoes (page 35). The Hutchison Library for bonfire kiln in Mali (page 7); Nigerian potter (page 8); wooden door in Nigeria (page 13); spinning cotton in Africa (page 24) and Kenyan woman basket weaving (page 36). The MacQuitty International Photographic Collection for Indian potter (page 8); heating glass (page 20); weaving with a back-strap loom (page 27) and American Indian basket (page 36). Museum of London for Roman sandals (page 35). Rietberg Museum, Zurich for African hippo box (page 19). The Board of Trustees of the Victoria and Albert Museum for Lucie Rie vase (page 9); Persian wall tile (page 10); dolphin chair (page 17) and Japanese inro (page 18).

The publishers would also like to give special thanks to Heather Kingsley-Heath and Gordon and Dorothy Whittle for the loan of items for photography and to Peter Hewlett for advice and for allowing himself to be photographed for the book.